TOSHI AND THE MISSING BALL-Y

DINA EZZEDDINE

Illustrated by Dani Saldaña

Toshi and the missing Ball-y. Copyright © 2023, 2024 by Dina Ezzeddine & Dani Saldana.

All rights reserved.

No portion of this book may be reproduced in any form without written permission from the publisher or author, except as permitted by Canada's copyright laws.

This publication is designed to provide accurate and authoritative information in regard to the subject matter covered. It is sold with the understanding that neither the author nor the publisher is engaged in rendering legal, investment, accounting or other professional services.

Cover Image and all Illustrations created by: Dani Saldana
Toshi and characters Story by: Dina Ezzeddine

Published by: Kindle Direct Publishing & IngramSpark, and all eBook platforms.

ISBN: 978-1-0688396-8-9 (softcover)
ISBN: 978-1-0688396-9-6 (hardcover)

Hi friends! Welcome! I'm so glad you came to play with me today! I am so happy to meet you! My name is **Toshi!** I am **5-years-old,** and I am a **Pomeranian.**

I live with my mom, and we live in **Canada.**

My mom is really cool, she spoils me a lot. She gets me so many treats, I never know what to do with them.

I live with three sisters, they're **coy fish! Sally, Polly and Molly!**

My best friend is **Pete!** He's a wiener dog.

I also have a friend who lives in our tree, he's a squirrel named **Squirrelly.**

I also have a favorite **ball!**

I call it **Ball-y** its yellow and hard and...

I like to... **nib, nib**
and
... **bite, bite** it all day long.

OHHHHHHH!
But something happened, **Ball-y** is missing and I can't find it anywhere.

I have searched everywhere for my...
...yellow **Ball-y**.

"Toshi!" mom said.

She opened the patio doors to put me outside.
It's warm outside today, and mom wants me to **play outside.**
I don't want to **play outside.** I want to sleep in my **bed inside.**

"Toshi!"
"Toshi!" said Squirrelly.

Squirrelly seems to be awake, he's very noisy in his tree.
I like **Squirrelly,** he's lived in our tree forever!
He's a talented squirrel.

"**Hi Squirrelly! Good morning!**" I said to him.

"**Good morning-ss Toshi,**" said Squirrelly.

"**Howdy-howdy-do today?**" Squirrelly sure has a weird way of talking.

But he's my friend and I like him. Even if he has a weird way of talking. Maybe I will ask him if he has seen **Ball-y.**

"**My mom is gone, and my Ball-y is gone! Have you seen my Ball-y?**" I asked him.

Squirrelly is a smart squirrel, he can find anything, and he loves nuts, he collects so many different kinds of nuts. His favorite is **ACORNS!**

"Toshi, your mom will be back, back-ity, back, back and so will Ball-y, ball, ball!" said Squirrelly.

OHHHHH!
But I miss my mom and my **Ball-y.**

"Toshi! Toshi! I have news, news, news," said Squirrelly.
I could barely understand what he was saying. I guess that's what makes him unique!

Oh I hope he found my **Ball-y.**

It's been missing ever since it rolled away months ago.

I hope he found it!
I'm so anxious to know
does Squirrelly know were it is?

SO...

SO...

LONG...

AGO!

"What news Squirrelly? What news?"

Oh what could it be. I am anxious now! Maybe its buried in a hole or maybe it's on Pete's side of the fence.

"I think, think-ity, think, think Ball-y is not lost, lost, lost..." said Squirrelly.

I AM SO EXCITED!!! Squirrelly says my ball is not lost.
I can't help myself, I am so excited.

This means **ball-y** is coming home. **I AM SO HAPPY!**

I've missed it so much, once it comes home I will...
...**nib, nib** and **bite, bite** it all day long.

"Where did you see Ball-y Squirrelly, where?" I asked.

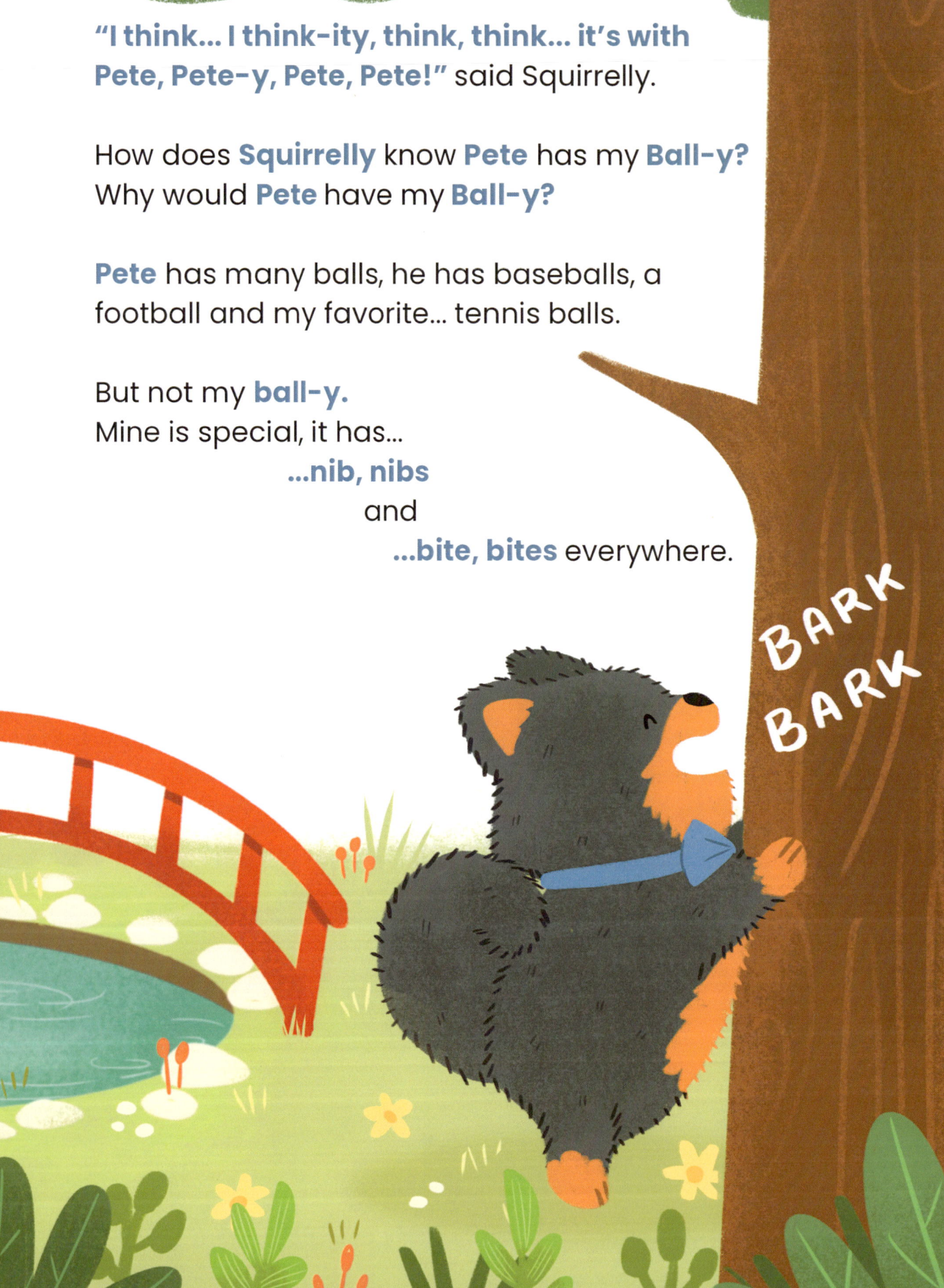

"I think... I think-ity, think, think... it's with **Pete, Pete-y, Pete, Pete!**" said Squirrelly.

How does **Squirrelly** know **Pete** has my **Ball-y?**
Why would **Pete** have my **Ball-y?**

Pete has many balls, he has baseballs, a football and my favorite... tennis balls.

But not my **ball-y.**
Mine is special, it has...
 ...nib, nibs
 and
  ...bite, bites everywhere.

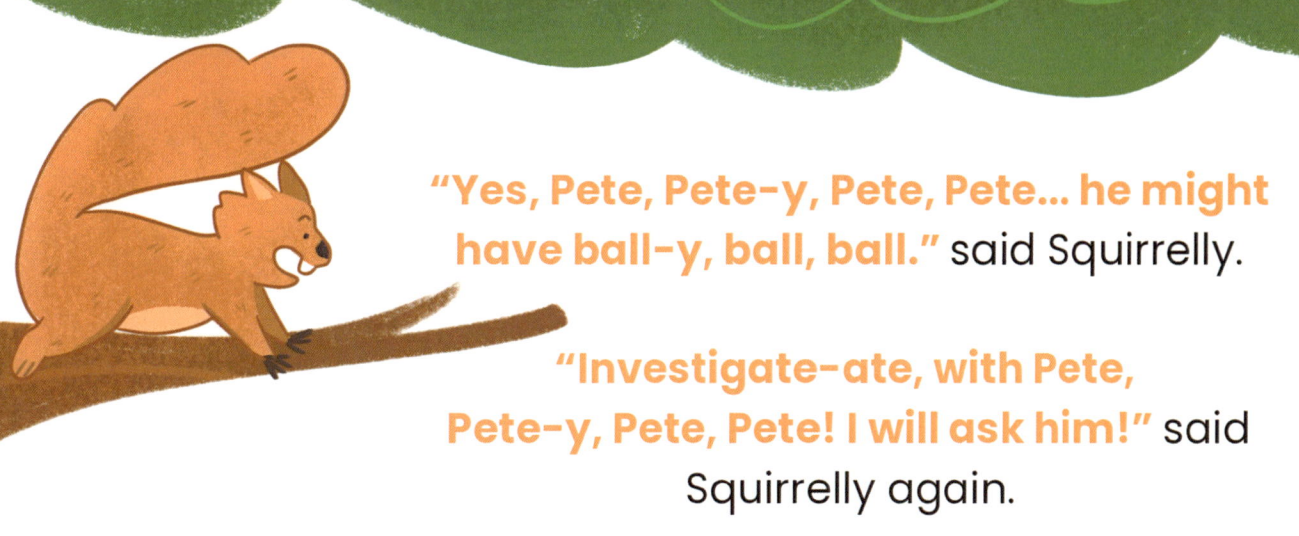

"Yes, Pete, Pete-y, Pete, Pete... he might have ball-y, ball, ball." said Squirrelly.

"Investigate-ate, with Pete, Pete-y, Pete, Pete! I will ask him!" said Squirrelly again.

How does **Squirrelly** climb like that?
He's so talented, he can climb anywhere and balance on anything, he can even balance on the fence that separates me from **Pete!**

I hope **Pete** has seen my **Ball-y!**

(Have you seen my **Ball-y** friends?
Do you see it anywhere?)

"Pete, Pete! Are you outside!"

I barked and barked, I hope **Pete** is awake and outside. Did his mom put him outside too? Where's **Pete**, is **Pete** outside yet!

"Pete, its Toshi!" I said.

"TOSHI! TOSHI…. I'm here TOSHI! I'm near the fence." Pete said.

He was awake and near the fence, I could hear him sniffing the ground for something. What was he looking for? I looked at **Squirrelly** and he was leaning over the fence on **Pete's** side.

"Pete… Pete-y, Pete, Pete!" Squirrelly said.

"Have you seen ball, ball-y, ball, ball?" Squirrelly asked Pete.

"What ball...whose ball...not my ball. My ball is in the ground, hiding. Whose ball Squirrelly?" said Pete.

Pete was still sniffing something on the ground when he said this.

I could hear Pete sniffing along the fence.

I didn't want his ball. I wanted my ball. Why did he think I wanted his ball?

My ball is best, it's a perfect ball. Its **yellow** and **round** and looks like a **bird-y-ball**. It's a perfect ball. I don't want **Pete's** ball.

"**Pete, Pete-y, Pete, Pete... Toshi, lost his ball-y, ball, ball**"
Squirrelly said.

He scurried down the other side of the fence. I couldn't see **Squirrelly** anymore, where did he go?

"**Ohhhhh, ball-y!**" Pete said.
He was still sniffing for something. What was he looking for?

"**Nope, no way! Not here... not here!**" Pete replied again.

OHHHH!
Pete doesn't know where it is either.
Now I'm even **sadder**. Its lost, lost forever! Where is **ball-y!**

"Not here, here-ity, here... right Pete, Pete-y, Pete?" said Squirrelly.

"No, why would it be here! I didn't see no ball-y! How did Toshi lose it?" Pete asked Squirrelly.

"Roll away, it rolled away, long, long ago. I searched every tree, tree-y, tree. No ball-y to be seen, seen, seen!" replied Squirrelly.

Maybe my sisters know where it is, I think I will ask them next.

"Molly, Polly, Sally are you awake!"

I am anxious to know, I hope my sisters saw my ball.
Maybe it's in their pond.
I hope they found **ball-y** or seen where it went.

Did it roll into their pond, or under the bridge or near the stone statues? Did **Squirrelly** hide it, or did **Molly, Polly and Sally** misplace it?

"Toshi, Toshi, Toshi!" they said.

"We're awake Toshi!" they said again.

"Hi Molly, Hi Polly and Hi Sally! Have you seen my ball-y?" I asked them.

"Ball-y, ball-y, ball-y?" each one of them said.
"Not here Toshi, not in our pond!" they all said at the same time.

"Oh, it's been missing for months and I can't find it!"

"It's not in our pond, Toshi! Ask Squirrelly!" all three of them said at the same time again.

I did ask **Squirrelly,** and he said he's investigating with **Pete.** Have you seen my **ball-y?**

"Strange, strange-y, strange, strange… its not with Pete!" Squirrelly said.

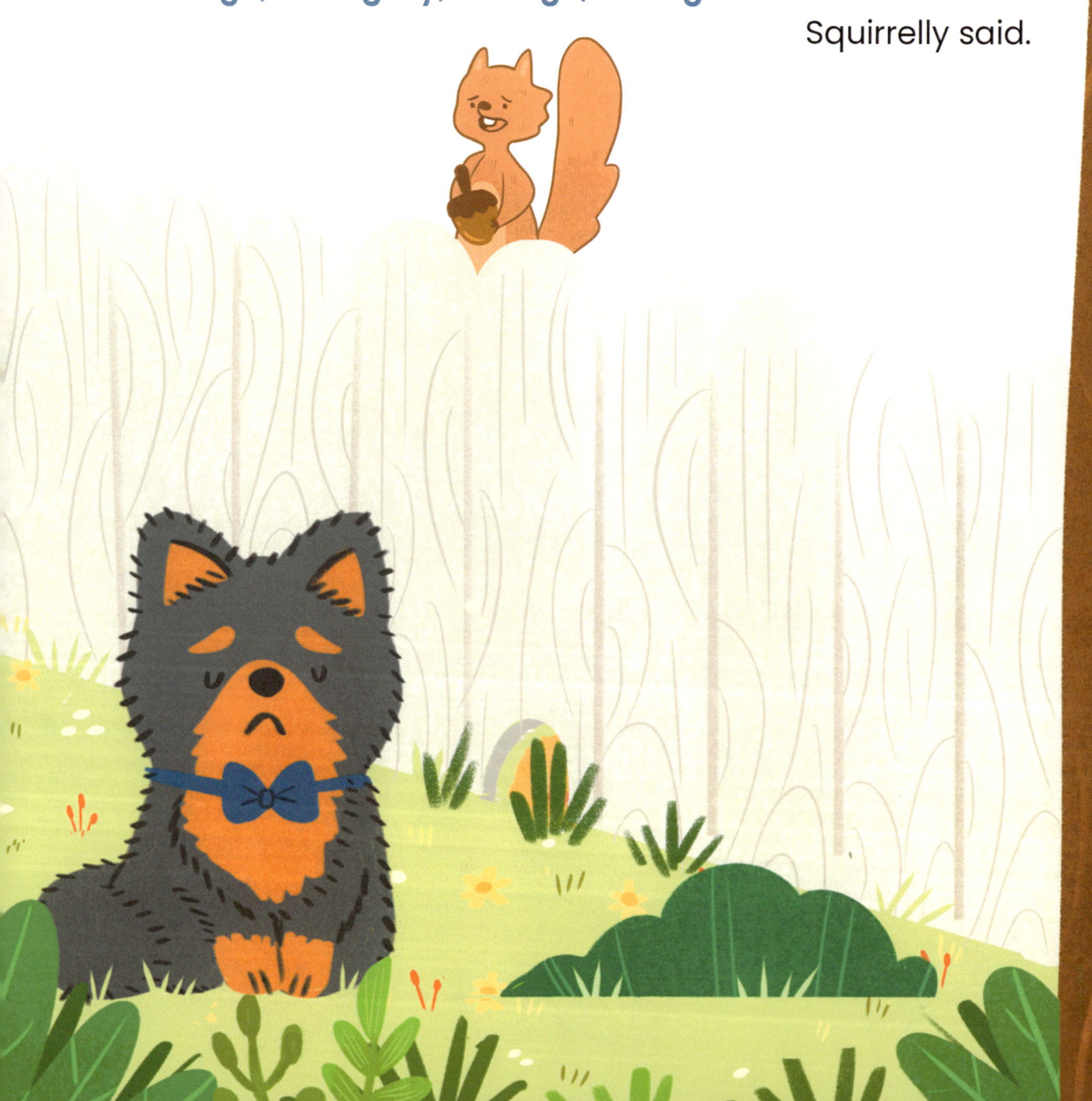

My heart was breaking now, my **ball-y** is **LOST** and maybe gone **FOREVER**.

Where is **ball-y?** Did anyone see **ball-y?**

"Hi, Squirrelly! Hi Toshi! Can we share your tree?" asked the birds.

Did I mention, we have five bird friends who come to visit us everyday, they're fun. I think they're sparrows.
I don't know, but they're my friends, and I like them.

Maybe they've seen **ball-y.** I will ask if they've seen **ball-y.** They fly everywhere, all over the place, maybe they spotted it somewhere.

"Birds, have you seen my ball-y!"
I asked the birds.

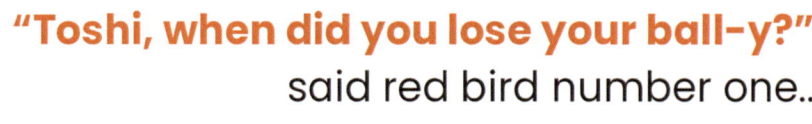

"Toshi, when did you lose your ball-y?" said red bird number one..

"Oh Bird! it's been missing for months. One day I had it, I was nib, nib, and bite, bite... here in the yard. And then mom called me inside and it rolled away. And I can't find it!" I told bird number one.

"Oh no Toshi! Oh no! We are your friends and we will help you find ball-y," said bird number one.

"We can help you find it, what's it looks like Toshi? Let's help you find it!" all the birds said this at the same time.

I was so happy my bird friends wanted to help me find **ball-y.** I have such good friends, they're so kind and so nice, they're always in our tree everyday and they love the snacks mom gives them too. I want to find my **ball-y** so badly, so I can share it with my friends.

"Birds, if you find ball-y, it is round and yellow, and looks like a bird, it has nib, nibs, and bite, bites on it… and it's so very special!" I said.

"We can look over head, up, up high in the sky. Come on birds lets fly!" said bird number one, who was perched on my head.

"Thank you, birds!" I replied to them.

They flew away from the tree, and up, up high they went. They'll for sure be able to see my ball so high in the sky.

"Toshi, Toshi! I'll help too!" said **Pete** from the other side of the fence.

Everyone will help find **ball-y,** I'm so excited. I can't contain myself. Let's find **ball-y** together.

Have you seen my **ball-y?** Can you find my **ball-y** friends?

"Toshi, I will sniff and sniff until I find ball-y! It shouldn't have gone far. I'll find it for you Toshi!" Pete said.

My tail would not stop wagging.
I was so excited that Pete was helping. Pete is a good boy, he always finds things that are hidden.

His yard is full of holes. Mom doesn't like the holes I make. She is always mad when I make holes. I hide treats in my holes. I don't know why she doesn't like my holes.

"I help-ity, help too Toshi! I scurry, scur-scurry, around the house, house-y, house, house. Maybe mom hid it somewhere… I'll be back in a quick-y, quick, quick second!" said Squirrelly.

"I will look in the yard! I will sniff, sniff until I smell it!" said Pete.

Ball-y has a special smell, it smells **special**, I can't tell you how it smells. But it has a **special** smell that only I will notice every time it's around. Do you have a special ball friends?

I bet your ball has a nice smell too. A special smell like my ball? Don't lose your ball if you have one friends, hide it and keep it safe!

"Toshi, Toshi!" My bird friends came back.
Did they find **ball-y?**

"Toshi! We searched up, up, up so high in the sky and we didn't see ball-y anywhere!" said the birds.

They perched on the house, and the bridge, and the statues. I sniffed again around my sister's pond, maybe I buried it somewhere.

"It's okay! Everyone is on a mission, and we'll find ball-y" I said to the birds.

"Toshi, Toshi!" my sisters said from the pond.

"We remember where ball-y went!" said Polly, Molly and Sally.

"Where? Where?" I asked.

ITS FOUND! Yay my sisters know where **ball-y** is. I knew it would be found.

"It's next to Pete. It rolled to Pete's side. Look Toshi, look at the hole in the fence…" Sally, Polly and Molly said.

"WOOOOHOOOOO! I FOUND BALL-Y."

"You're such a good boy Toshi," mom said.

Remember to always share with your friends, when you get new toys!

I gave my friends, all my new balls, because they helped me find my special **ball-y!**

◯ author_illustratordina
✉ aiko10195@gmail.com
f missDinaAuthor

Leave us a Review!
⭐⭐⭐⭐⭐

About the Author

Dina Ezzeddine is a Canadian writer of children's books and adventure novels. Along with the talented artistic skills of Dani Saldana, they created the story of Toshi together. You can find Toshi's adventures at Dina's social Media pages.

Illustrated by Dani Saldaña

Bē www.behance.net/danisaldana
◯ daniii.saldana
✉ hello.danisaldana@gmail.com

www.ingramcontent.com/pod-product-compliance
Lightning Source LLC
Chambersburg PA
CBRC090838010526
44118CB00007B/247